1992.

THE GOURMET QUOTATION BOOK

By the same author

The Wine Quotation Book

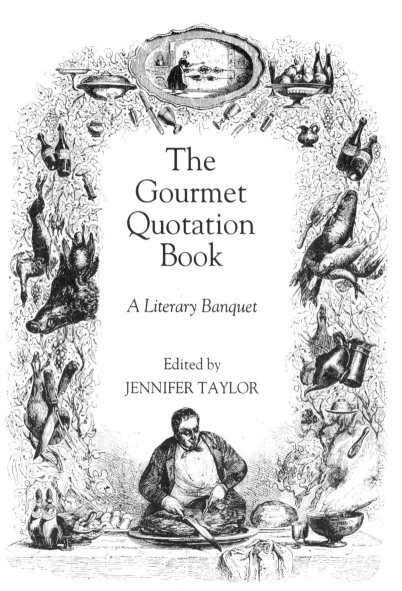

The Gourmet Quotation Book

A Literary Banquet

Edited by
JENNIFER TAYLOR

ROBERT HALE · LONDON

ISBN 0 7090 4146 2

Robert Hale Limited
Clerkenwell House
Clerkenwell Green
London EC1R 0HT

Photoset in Goudy by
Derek Doyle & Associates
Printed and bound in Hong Kong

Preface

 This catalogue of succulent roasts, exquisite fish and luscious fruit enjoyed down the centuries will not go down well with the abstemious, anyone on a diet or those who consider enjoyment in food reprehensible.

There is also the issue of quantity. With current strictures on healthy eating, there are constant exhortations in the press, in articles of the 'We all eat too much' variety, to have a little plainly grilled fish with a side salad – fare which the monks of old would certainly have considered mortified the flesh. One does not do much better with the parsimonious helpings and pretensions of nouvelle cuisine. Gross overeating there most obviously was in previous centuries, but a table of plenty did not necessarily lead to excess.

The definition of the word 'gourmet' as a connoisseur of food is relatively new (until the early nineteenth century it meant a wine-taster's assistant). Holding sway in the centuries before that was the French word gourmand, which the English soon translated as 'greedy' or even 'gluttonous'; Randle Cotgrave, for instance, in his 1611 dictionary defined it as 'bellie-god' or 'gully-gut', and later Dr Johnson (no mean eater himself) gave the meaning of 'gormand' as 'a ravenous luxurious feeder'. But the word lost its connotations of greed in France, where eating well is a natural part of life, and there is nothing disreputable about being a gourmand – on the contrary.

5

Preface

As with wine, it is the British who, when knowledgeable, tend to become a trifle pretentious, and the word 'gourmet' now seems to have slightly precious overtones. For the purposes of this book I have taken it to mean one who is discriminating about quality and enjoys good food and wine; I see no reason why he should not be endowed with both gusto and commonsense, as well as a sense of proportion, and I would not like him to have the earnest obsessiveness of a foodie.

As James Beard once remarked, it should be a matter not of 'gourmet' cooking but of good cooking. Tastes and foodstuffs are varied, and as our gourmet is not precious he does not restrict himself to quenelles de brochet à la mousseline de homard. Exquisite fumets de poisson have their place, of course, but so do a well-cooked stew, a dish of bacon and eggs, and home-made bread. All is in the quality of the ingredients.

Many of the passages simply celebrate the fruits of the earth. Restaurateur Sally Clarke was quoted in a Times interview last year as saying that she considered it important for her staff to have been to Italy and 'smelt the olives'. I would add to that the smell of sun-drenched apricots and peaches straight from the tree.

And so to this celebration of 'good things'. There is something for every taste, from the delicate flavours of gleaming, freshly caught fish to the richness of gamey game. Call it a literary binge if you like. But many are the writers to attest to the well-being induced by good food. Could not some of this mellow benevolence act as an antidote in a stress-ridden, anxious world?

JENNIFER TAYLOR

Man could direct his ways by plain reason and support his life by tasteless food; but God has given us wit, and flavour, and brightness and laughter.

    REVD SYDNEY SMITH
    Dangers and Advantages of Wit

Every man should eat and drink, and enjoy the good of all his labour; it is the gift of God.

    ECCLESIASTES, 3:13

First parents of the human race, whose *gourmandise* is historical, and who lost all for an apple, what would you not have done for a truffled turkey?

    BRILLAT-SAVARIN
    La Physiologie du goût

All food is the gift of the gods and has something of the miraculous, the egg no less than the truffle.

    SYBILLE BEDFORD

Acorns were good till bread was found.
> JUVENAL
> *Satires*

In general, mankind, since the improvement of cookery,
eat twice as much as nature requires.
> BENJAMIN FRANKLIN

Who satisfieth thy mouth with good things; so that thy
youth is renewed like the eagle's.
> PSALMS, 103:5

Gourmandise presents itself with a thoroughly theological
face. By divine right, man is the king of nature, and
everything that the earth produces has been created for
him.
> BRILLAT-SAVARIN
> *La Physiologie du goût*

He lived for the pleasures of the flesh,
for he was Epicurus' own son,
and ever claimed that perfect happiness
lay in the art of pleasing the palate ...
His bread and beer were of the very best,
and no one ever kept a finer cellar.
His house was never without cooked food –
both fish and meat – and held in such abundance
that it snowed meat and drink indoors
with all the fancy foods one could imagine.

With every passing season of the year,
he'd order different dishes to appear.
He'd many a fine fat partridge in his coops
and many bream and pike swam in his pond.
> CHAUCER
> *The Canterbury Tales*
> description of the Franklin

Gourmand: a glutton, gormand, bellie-god, greedie-gut; a
great eater, monstrous feeder, gully-gut.
> RANDLE COTGRAVE
> *A Dictionarie of the French and English Tongues*, 1611

I have looked up the word *Gourmandise* in all the
dictionaries, and I am far from satisfied with what I have
found. Confusion persists between *gourmandise* in its true
sense, and *gluttony* or *voracity*, and I conclude from this that
lexicographers, worthy men though they may be in other
respects, are not to be found among those amiable scholars
who gracefully pick up a partridge wing with their little
finger crooked, and wash it down with a glass of Lafite or
Clos-Vougeot.
> BRILLAT-SAVARIN
> *La Physiologie du goût*

It only requires a voracious appetite to be a glutton. It
demands an exquisite judgment, a profound knowledge of
every branch of the culinary art, a sensual and delicate
palate, and a thousand other qualities very difficult to
combine, in order to merit the title of gourmand.
> GRIMOD DE LA REYNIÈRE
> *Almanach des gourmands*

Only fools are not gourmands. Being a gourmand is like being an artist, a scholar, a poet.... To lack a sense of taste is to lack an exquisite faculty, that of appreciating the qualities of food.

GUY DE MAUPASSANT
Le Rosier de Madame Husson

Where is the fool or the man of genius that is insensible to the charms of a good dinner?

W.M. THACKERAY
Miscellaneous Papers

Do you think that God made good things only for fools?

DESCARTES
on being asked about his fondness for sweet things

At the inn where we stopped he was exceedingly dissatisfied with some roast mutton which we had for dinner. The ladies I saw wondered to see the great philosopher, whose wisdom and wit they had been admiring all the way, get into ill-humour from such a cause. He scolded the waiter, saying, 'It is as bad as bad can be: it is ill-fed, ill-killed, ill-kept, and ill-drest.'

JAMES BOSWELL
Life of Johnson

The gourmand is always happy and cheerful. He is always in a state of pleasant well-being. The gourmand is in harmony with the outside world. He is in fact a normal person.

EDOUARD DE POMIANE
Cooking with Pomiane

After eating, an *epicure* gives a thin smile of satisfaction; a *gastronome*, burping into his napkin, praises the food in a magazine; a *gourmet*, repressing his burp, criticizes the food in the same magazine; a *gourmand* belches happily and tells everybody where he ate.

WILLIAM SAFIRE
New York Times, January 1985

I am a gourmet
YOU are a gourmand
HE is fat

CRAIG BROWN
The Times, November 1989

A gourmet is just a glutton with brains.

PHILIP W. HABERMAN
Vogue, January 1961

... usually little more than a glutton festooned with charge cards.

SYDNEY J. HARRIS

I have never been anything so refined as a *gourmet*; so I am happy to say that I am still quite capable of being a glutton. My ignorance of cookery is such that I can even eat the food in the most fashionable and expensive hotels in London.

G.K. CHESTERTON
Autobiography

If some people are born to be gourmands, others become so by nature of their profession, and I am able to list here four main groups: financiers, doctors, men of letters and the devout.

> BRILLAT-SAVARIN
> *La Physiologie du goût*

Gourmandise, the sin of virtuous monks

> HONORÉ DE BALZAC
> *Le Cousin Pons*

The monastery at Alcobaca
The three prelates led the way to, I verily believe, the most distinguished temple of gluttony in all Europe.... My eyes never beheld in any modern convent of France, Italy, or Germany, such an enormous space dedicated to culinary purposes. Through the centre of the immense and nobly groined hall ... ran a brisk rivulet of the clearest water, containing every sort and size of the finest river fish. On one side loads of game and venison were heaped up, on the other vegetables and fruit in endless variety ... hillocks of wheaten flour whiter than snow, rocks of sugar, jars of the finest oil, and pastry in vast abundance, which a numerous tribe of lay brothers and their attendants were rolling out and puffing up into an hundred different shapes, singing all the while as blithely as larks in a cornfield....

'There,' said the Lord Abbot, 'we shall not starve: God's bounties are great, it is fit we should enjoy them.'

> WILLIAM BECKFORD
> *Travel Diaries*

I have consorted with epicures of all ages and nations, but I never saw men who relished a dinner better than the learned fellows of St Boniface.

W.M. THACKERAY
Miscellaneous Papers

'Your Majesty has an excellent appetite, as I have already had the honour of mentioning, but you select what you eat with too much refinement to be called a great eater.'

ALEXANDRE DUMAS
Porthos to Louis XIV in
Le Vicomte de Bragelonne

Not only was he remarkable for the extraordinary quantity which he eat, but he was, or affected to be, a man of very nice discernment in the science of cookery. He used to descant critically on the dishes which had been at table where he had dined or supped, and to recollect very minutely what he had liked.

JAMES BOSWELL
Life of Johnson

In their palate alone is their reason of existence.

JUVENAL
Satires

Foodies are *all* palate, with a vestigial person attached.

ANN BARR and PAUL LEVY
The Official Foodie Handbook

How disenchanting in the female character is a manifestation of relish for the pleasures of the table!
WILLIAM CHARLES MACREADY
Reminiscences, 1875

There is no more charming sight than a pretty *gourmande* in action: her napkin is placed to best advantage; one hand rests on the table, while the other conveys to her mouth elegant morsels, or a wing of partridge....
BRILLAT-SAVARIN
La Physiologie du goût

Enchant, stay beautiful and gracious; but to do this, eat well. Bring the same consideration to the preparation of your food as you devote to your appearance. Let your dinner be a poem, like your dress.
CHARLES MONSELET
Lettres à Emilie

There is something instinctive in the taste which the fair sex has for *gourmandise*, for it is favourable to beauty.... A succulent, delicate and careful diet delays the outward signs of old age for a long time. It makes the eyes shine, the skin bloom, and the muscles firmer.... All things being equal, those who know how to eat look ten years younger than those who are ignorant of that science.
BRILLAT-SAVARIN
La Physiologie du goût

To care for oneself by drinking excellent wines and by eating excellent dishes – that is the proper, the true medication.
> M. CHÂTILLON-PLESSIS
> *La Vie à table*, 1894

At the age of eighty, I eat oysters every morning, I dine well, and I do pretty well for supper; heroes are made for a lesser merit than mine.
> SAINT-ÉVREMONT
> in a letter to Ninon de Lenclos

Taking food and drink is a great enjoyment for healthy people, and those who do not enjoy eating seldom have much capacity for enjoyment or usefulness of any sort.
> CHARLES W. ELIOT
> *The Happy Life*

Eating well gives a spectacular joy to life.
> ELSA SCHIAPARELLI
> *Shocking Life*

One cannot think well, love well, sleep well, if one has not dined well.
> VIRGINIA WOOLF
> *A Room of One's Own*

He that eateth well, drinketh well; he that drinketh well, sleepeth well; he that sleepeth well, sinneth not; he that sinneth not goeth straight through Purgatory to Paradise.
>WILLIAM LITHGOW
>*Rare Adventures*, 1614

Dr Middleton misdoubted the future as well as the past of the man who did not, in becoming gravity, exult to dine. That man he deemed unfit for this world and the next.
>GEORGE MEREDITH
>*The Egoist*

Show me another pleasure like dinner which comes every day and lasts an hour.
>TALLEYRAND

Sir, Respect Your Dinner: idolize it, enjoy it properly. You will be many hours in the week, many weeks in the year, and many years in your life happier if you do.
>W.M. THACKERAY

The joys of the table are superior to all other pleasures, notably those of personal adornment, of drinking and of love, and those procured by perfumes and by music.
>HASSAN EL BAGHDADI
>*Kitabe el-tabih*, 1226

Good dinners are so much rarer than good women: and far more piquant.

> G.B. BURGIN
> *Which Woman?*

Kissing don't last: cookery do.

> GEORGE MEREDITH
> *The Ordeal of Richard Feverel*

Some singers sing of women's eyes,
And some of women's lips ...
Yet I, though custom call me crude,
Prefer to sing in praise of food.

> OGDEN NASH
> 'The Clean Platter' in *The Face is Familiar*

... is there a woman, however beautiful, who is worth those admirable red partridges of Languedoc.... Can one compare a pretty, simpering face with these splendid sheep of the Ardennes ... whose flesh fairly melts in one's mouth?

> GRIMOD DE LA REYNIÈRE
> *Mon Abnégation*

Editor's note: It seems that Madame Grimod was of rather sour disposition.

After a perfect meal, we are more susceptible to the ecstasy of love than at any other time.

> HANS BAZLI

A good meal soothes the soul as it regenerates the body. From the abundance of it flows a benign benevolence.

> FREDERICK W. HACKWOOD
> *Good Cheer*, 1911

After a good dinner, one can forgive anybody, even one's own relations.

> OSCAR WILDE
> *A Woman of No Importance*

I have yet to meet the man who, with a good *tournedos Rossini* inside him, was not the finer for it.

> CLIFTON FADIMAN

Madame, I have only cried twice in my life; once when I dropped a wing of truffled chicken into Lake Como, and once, when for the first time I heard you sing.

> ROSSINI to the singer Adelina Patti

I have been a great observer and I can truly say that I have never known a man 'fond of good eating and drinking', as it is called, … who was not worthy of respect.

> WILLIAM COBBETT
> *Advice to Young Men*, 1829

I hate a man who swallows it [food], affecting not to know what he is eating. I suspect his taste in higher matters.

> CHARLES LAMB
> *Essays of Elia*

'She should be thinking of higher things.'
  'Nothing could be higher than food,' said Leah.
    IVY COMPTON-BURNETT
    The Mighty and Their Fall

What is literature compared with cooking? The one is shadow, the other is substance.
    E.V. LUCAS
    365 Days and One More

When we no longer have good cooking in the world, we will have no literature, nor high and sharp intelligence, nor friendly gatherings, nor social harmony.
    MARIE-ANTOINE CARÊME

Bad cooks – and the utter lack of reason in the kitchen – have delayed human development longest and impaired it most.
    NIETZSCHE
    Beyond Good and Evil

A good cook is the peculiar gift of the gods. He must be a perfect creature from the brain to the palate, from the palate to the finger's end.
    WALTER SAVAGE LANDOR
    Imaginary Conversations

The true cook holds in his palm the happiness of mankind.
NORMAN DOUGLAS
South Wind

A good cook is like a sorceress who dispenses happiness.
ELSA SCHIAPARELLI
Shocking Life

What does cookery mean? It means the knowledge of Medea and of Circe, and of Calypso, and Sheba. It means knowledge of all herbs, and fruits, and balms and spices, and of all that is healing and sweet in grapes and savoury in meat.... It means the economy of your great-grandmother and the science of modern chemistry, and French art, and Arabian hospitality. It means, in fine, that you are to see imperatively that everyone has something nice to eat.
JOHN RUSKIN

You want to spread a little happiness, *non?*
PAUL BOCUSE
quoted in *The Sunday Times*, October 1989

No mean woman can cook well. It calls for a generous spirit, a light hand and a large heart.
EDEN PHILLPOTTS

Some people's food always tastes better than others, even if they are cooking the same dish ... because one person has much more life in them – more fire, more vitality, more guts – than others.
ROSA LEWIS
British hotelier

The most indispensable ingredient of all good home cooking: love for those you are cooking for.
SOPHIA LOREN

It scarcely bears thinking about, the time and labour that man and womankind has devoted to the preparation of dishes that are to melt and vanish in a moment like smoke or a dream.
ROSE MACAULAY
Personal Pleasures

Cuisine is like a fireworks display, nothing remains. It is *une fête*, rapid, ephemeral.
PAUL BOCUSE
quoted in *The Listener*, 1976

Cookery is an art still changing, and of momentary triumph. Know on *thyself* thy genius must depend. All books of cookery, all helps of art are vain, if void of genius thou wouldst cook.
ATHENAEUS

Cookery is not chemistry. It is an art. It requires instinct and taste rather than exact measurements.
MARCEL BOULESTIN
Petits et grands plats

A cook is creative, marrying ingredients in the way a poet marries words.
ROGER VERGÉ
Cuisine of the Sun
translated by Caroline Conran

Recipe cooking is to real cooking as painting by number is to real painting: just pretend.

> JOHN THORNE
> *Simple Cooking*

The kitchen is territory where there are always discoveries to be made.

> GRIMOD DE LA REYNIÈRE
> *Almanach des gourmands*

To do justice to the science and research of a dinner so served would require a knowledge of the art equal to that which produced it.

> LADY MORGAN
> on a dinner cooked by Carême in 1828

The destiny of nations depends on what they eat.

> FRENCH PROVERB

I am more in need of saucepans than written instructions.

> TALLEYRAND to Louis XVIII at the time of the Congress of Vienna

Skilful and refined cookery has always been a feature of the most glorious epochs in history.

> LUCIEN TENDRET
> *La Table au pays de Brillat-Savarin*

In the number of dishes and changes of meat, the nobility of England (whose cooks for the most part are musical-headed Frenchmen and strangers) do most exceed, sith there is not a day in manner passeth over their heads wherein they have not only beef, mutton, veal and lamb, kid, pork, coney, capon, pig or so many of these that the season yieldeth, but also some portion of the red and fallow deer, besides a great variety of fish and wild fowl, and thereto sundry other delicacies.

    HOLINSHED
    Chronicle of England, 1577

If I had my health ... I would request his company to the tenant's feast at my own table, and show him, if he is too young a man to remember, what an old English table was when we were too wise to run after foreign gewgaws, and were content with the best of everything, dressed in the English fashion by English people.

    CHARLOTTE SMITH
    The Old Manor House, 1793

Sauce à la Tartare opened to me a new train of ideas. How shall I be able to live upon the large raw limbs of meat to which I am destined? Where shall I find those delicious stews, that thoroughly subjugated meat which opposes no resistance to the teeth, and still preserves all the gravies for the palate? It fills me with despair and remorse to think how badly I have been fed, and how my time has been misspent and wasted on bread sauce and melted butter.

    REVD SYDNEY SMITH
    in a letter to a friend in Yorkshire

Never was there such a take in. I had been given to understand that his Lordship's cuisine was superintended by the first French artists, and that I should find there all the luxuries of the *Almanach des Gourmands*. What a mistake! His Lordship is luxurious, indeed, but in quite a different way. He is a true Englishman.... A huge haunch of venison on the side-board; a magnificent piece of beef at the bottom of the table; and before my Lord himself smoked, not a *dindon aux truffes*, but a fat roasted goose, stuffed with sage and onions. I was disappointed.

THOMAS MACAULAY
after dining with Lord Essex

We greatly surpass the French in mutton, we produce better beef, lamb, and pork, and are immeasurably superior both in the quantity and quality of our fish, our venison, and our game, yet we cannot compare, as a nation, with the higher, the middle, or the lower classes in France in the science of preparing our daily food. The only articles of food in the quality of which the French surpass us are veal and fowl, but such is the skill and science of their cooks that with worse mutton, worse beef, and worse lamb than ours, they produce better chops, cutlets, steaks, and better-made dishes of every nature and kind whatsoever. In *fricassées*, *ragoûts*, *salmis*, *quenelles*, *purées*, *filets*, and more especially in the dressing of vegetables, our neighbours surpass us.

JOSEPH BREGION and ANNE MILLER
The Practical Cook, 1845

Why should not *all* classes participate in the benefit to be derived from nourishment calculated to sustain healthfully the powers of life? And why should the English, as a people, remain more ignorant than their continental neighbours of so simple a matter as that of preparing it for themselves?

    ELIZA ACTON
    Modern Cookery for Private Families, 1845

The English ideal of cooking is the best in the world ... to give each article of food its own especial flavour. The drawback is that England has scarcely any cooks, and so it is seldom you find their ideals carried out.

    FRANK HARRIS
    My Life and Loves

One symptom of the decline of culture in Britain is indifference to the art of preparing food.

    T.S. ELIOT
    Notes Towards the Definition of Culture, 1948

Dining is the privilege of civilization.... The nation which knows how to dine has learnt the leading lesson of progress.

    ISABELLA BEETON
    The Book of Household Management, 1861

Everything ends this way in France – everything. Weddings, christenings, duels, funerals, swindlings, diplomatic affairs – everything is a pretext for a good dinner.

    JEAN ANOUILH
    Cécile

'It seems strange that we country people try to eat up our food as quickly as possible, so as to get back to work, while here we are doing our best to linger over lunch, and with that in mind eating oysters …'

'But of course,' countered Stepan Arkadyevich, 'that's just the aim of civilization – to create pleasure out of everything.'

> LEO TOLSTOY
> *Anna Karenina*

The art of dining well is no slight art, the pleasure not a slight pleasure.

> MONTAIGNE
> *Essais*

Food should be sniffed lustily at table … the sniffing of it to be regarded in the same light as the tasting of it.

> E.B. WHITE
> *Every Day Is Saturday*

A dog will carry his bone to a private nook and do his gnawing undisturbed, but civilized man wants companions who can talk, to nourish his mind as well as his body.

> JOHN ERSKINE
> *The Complete Life*

The conversation now began to be little more than a rhapsody of exclamations; as each had pretty well satisfied his own appetite, he now found sufficient time to press others. 'Excellent, the very thing; let me recommend the pig; do but taste the bacon; never eat a better thing in my life; exquisite, delicious.'

> OLIVER GOLDSMITH
> *The Citizen of the World*

Do not be afraid to talk about food. Food which is worth eating is worth discussing.

> MARCEL BOULESTIN
> *Simple French Cooking for English Homes*

I shall not easily forget a Matelotte at the Rocher de Cancale, an almond tart at Montreuil, or a Poulet à la Tartare at Grignon's.... These are impressions which no changes in future life can ever obliterate.

> REVD SYDNEY SMITH
> in a letter from Paris to Lady Grey, 1835

In default of substantial banquets even imaginary ones are pleasant.... What a fine, manly, wholesome sense of roast and boiled, so to speak, there is in the *Iliad*! ... that venison pasty in *Quentin Durward*, of the flavour of which I have the most distinct notion, and to which I never sit down without appetite, nor quite unsatisfied.

> W.M. THACKERAY
> *Miscellaneous Papers*

More than one escaped war prisoner has told me of the strange peacefulness that will come over a group of near-famished men in their almost endless talk of good food they remember.

>M.F.K. FISHER
>*An Alphabet for Gourmets*

O, blissful recollections of that dinner! ... Lonely and sorrowful as I now sit, digesting with many a throe the iron thews of a British beefsteak ... I see the grateful apparitions of *Escallopes de Saumon* and *Laitances de Carpes* rise in a gentle vapour before my eyes.

>EDWARD BULWER-LYTTON
>*Pelham*

'Where's the use of titivating one's appetite with reading of such luxteries? ... Oh! dear, oh! dear, I shall die of hunger I see – I shall die of absolute famine, my stomach thinks my throat's cut already.'

>R.S. SURTEES
>*Jorrocks' Jaunts and Jollities*

Appetite is the best sauce.

>FRENCH PROVERB

The best sauce in the world is hunger.

>CERVANTES
>*Don Quixote*

If you have been taking too many plovers' eggs, or *foie-gras* patty, for breakfast, if you feel yourself a trifle heavy or incommoded after a hot luncheon, you naturally mount your cob, take a gentle breathing for a couple of hours on the Blenheim or Bagley road, and return to dress for dinner at the last minute; still feeling that you have not got your appetite quite back.... In this case ... take my advice.... Spend twenty minutes in your easy chair over the *Practical Cook*. Begin almost at any page. After the first few paragraphs the languor and heaviness begin to disappear. The idea of dining, which was quite disagreeable to you half an hour since, begins to be no longer repulsive....

    W.M. THACKERAY
    Miscellaneous Papers

A stomach that is seldom empty despises common food.

    HORACE
    Satires

After delicious fare I take no common food.

    PETRONIUS
    Satyricon

I make it my rule to consume very limited quantities of plain food in order to leave as much room as possible for delicacies.

    E.V. KNOX
    Gorgeous Times

Delicacies are apt to satiate the appetite, and to produce such a whimsical craving after novelty, as to render the coarsest food unpalatable. The most luxurious Epicures sometimes prescribe to themselves abstinence, in order to excite the greater relish for an expected dainty.

JANE WEST
A Gossip's Story, 1797

Novelty! It is the prevailing cry; it is imperiously demanded by everyone.... What feats of ingenuity have we not been forced to perform ... to meet our customers' wishes?

AUGUSTE ESCOFFIER
A Guide to Modern Cookery

I want a dish to taste good, rather than to have been seethed in pig's milk and served wrapped in a rhubarb leaf with grated thistle root.

KINGSLEY AMIS
London Illustrated News, May 1986

I have four thousand cookbooks dating back to 1503 and everything that is in 'nouvelle cuisine' was there two hundred years ago.

ANTON MOSIMANN
Now! magazine, 1981

People have been cooking and eating for thousands of years, so if you are the very first to have thought of adding fresh lime juice to scalloped potatoes try to understand that there must be a reason for this.

FRAN LEBOWITZ
Metropolitan Life

People pretend to enjoy picturesque combinations that don't make culinary sense.

> EGON RONAY, writing about nouvelle cuisine
> *The Sunday Times*, October 1989

The so-called nouvelle cuisine usually means not enough on your plate and too much on your bill.

> PAUL BOCUSE
> quoted in *The Evening Standard*, 1985

'Cuisine heureuse', which consists of marrying natural products with one another, ... is the antithesis of cooking to impress.

> ROGER VERGÉ
> *Cuisine of the Sun*
> translated by Caroline Conran

I don't like gourmet cooking or 'this' cooking or 'that' cooking. I like *good* cooking.

> JAMES BEARD
> *Newsweek*, 1985

A cook ... should be a judge of the season of every dish, as well as know perfectly the state of every article he undertakes to prepare.

> ISABELLA BEETON
> *The Book of Household Management*, 1861

Our meals ... reflected both the rhythm of the seasons and the incidents of Françoise's life – a brill, because the fish-woman had vouched for its freshness; a turkey, because she had seen a beautiful one in the market at Roussainville-le-Pin; cardoons with marrow, because she had never done them for us that way before; a roast leg of lamb, because the fresh air gave us an appetite ...; spinach, by way of a change; apricots, because they were still scarce; gooseberries, because they would be over in a fortnight's time; raspberries, because M. Swann had brought some over.

> MARCEL PROUST
> *Du Côté de chez Swann*

Cooking should be a carefully balanced reflection of all the good things of the earth.

> JEAN and PIERRE TROISGROS
> *The Nouvelle Cuisine of Jean and Pierre Troisgros*
> translated by Caroline Conran

Why has our poetry eschewed
The rapture and response of food?
What hymns are sung and praises said
For the home-made miracle of bread?

> LOUIS UNTERMEYER

Talk of joy: there may be things better than beef stew and baked potatoes and home-made bread – there may be.

> DAVID GRAYSON
> *Adventures in Contentment*

Gentle bakers, make good bread! For good bread doth comfort, confirm and doth establish a man's heart, beside the properties rehearsed.

> ANDREW BOORDE
> *A Dyetary of Helth*, 1542

The peasants of Sicily, who have kept their own wheat and make their own natural brown bread, ah, it is amazing how fresh and sweet and *clean* their loaf seems, so perfumed, as home-made bread used all to be before the war.

> D.H. LAWRENCE
> *Sea and Sardinia*

Her corn-cake, in all its varieties of hoe-cake, dodgers, muffins, and other species ... was a sublime mystery to all less practiced compounders.

> HARRIET BEECHER STOWE
> *Uncle Tom's Cabin*

The angels in Paradise eat nothing but *vermicelli al pomidoro*.

> DUKE OF BOVINO
> Mayor of Naples, in 1930

In China we have only three religions, but we have a hundred dishes we can make from rice.

> CHINESE PROVERB

I had an excellent repast – the best repast possible – which consisted simply of boiled eggs and bread and butter. It was the quality of these simple ingredients that made the occasion memorable. The eggs were so good that I am ashamed to say how many of them I consumed.... It might seem that an egg which has succeeded in being fresh has done all that can reasonably be expected of it. But there was a bloom of punctuality, so to speak, about these eggs of Bourg, as if it had been the intention of the very hens themselves that they should be promptly served.

> HENRY JAMES
> *A Little Tour in France*

Give good heed to serve eggs of an oblong shape, for they have a better flavour and are whiter than the round; they are firm and enclose a male yolk.

> HORACE
> *Satires*

The still hissing bacon and the eggs that looked like tufts of primroses ...

> BENJAMIN DISRAELI
> *Coningsby*

Who can help loving a land that has taught us six hundred and eighty-five ways to dress eggs?

> THOMAS MOORE
> *The Fudge Family in Paris*, 1818

Mère Poulard's omelette
Here is the recipe for the omelette: I break some good eggs
in a bowl, I beat them well, I put a good lump of butter in
the pan, I pour in the eggs and I stir them constantly. I am
happy, monsieur, if this recipe pleases you.

> MÈRE POULARD
> of Mont-St-Michel, famous for her omelettes, in a
> letter, June 1922

The curé's tuna omelette
The omelette was round, bulging, and done to a turn. As
the spoon broke into it, delectable and fragrant juices ran
out of the paunch and seemed to fill the plate.

> BRILLAT-SAVARIN
> *La Physiologie du goût*

He discovered that an omelette was much lighter when the
whites were not beaten together with the yolks with the
usual force that cooks put into the operation. The trick
was, according to him, to froth up the whites into a
mousse, and only then gradually blend in the yolks.

> HONORÉ DE BALZAC
> *La Rabouilleuse*

These are the beasts which ye shall eat: the ox, the sheep,
and the goat.

The hart, and the roebuck, and the fallow deer, and the
wild goat, and the pygarg, and the wild ox, and the
chamois.

And every beast that parteth the hoof, and cleaveth the
cleft into two claws, and cheweth the cud among the
beasts, that ye shall eat.

> DEUTERONOMY, 14:4–6

And as for excellent good Beef and Veale, there is no countrie in the world that can parallel, farre less exceed our beeves and veale here in England, whatsoever some talke of Hungary and Poland.

HART
The Diet of the Diseased, 1633

The quality of the flesh of an animal is considerably influenced by the nature of the *food on which it has been fed*; for the food supplies the material which produces the flesh. If the food be not suitable and good, the meat cannot be good either.

ISABELLA BEETON
The Book of Household Management, 1861

The nearer the bone, the sweeter the flesh.

ENGLISH PROVERB

No man eat more heartily than Johnson, or loved better what was nice and delicate. Mr Wilkes was very assiduous in helping him to some fine veal. 'Pray give me leave, Sir: – It is better here – A little of the brown – Some fat, Sir – A little of the stuffing – Some gravy – Let me have the pleasure of giving you some butter – Allow me to recommend a squeeze of this orange; – or the lemon, perhaps, may have more zest.'

JAMES BOSWELL
Life of Johnson

Since for her nothing was more important than the basic quality of the ingredients, ... Françoise would go to the Halles herself to select the finest pieces of rump steak, shins of beef, and calves' feet, just as Michelangelo spent eight months in Carrara selecting the most perfect blocks of marble for the monument of Julius II.

MARCEL PROUST
Du Côté de chez Swann

... a mighty porterhouse steak an inch and a half thick, hot and sputtering from the griddle; dusted with fragrant pepper; enriched with little melting bits of butter of the most unimpeachable freshness and genuineness; the precious juices of the meat trickling out and joining the gravy, archipelagoed with mushrooms....

MARK TWAIN
A Tramp Abroad

A daube cooked gently in an earthenware casserole of venerable age, for three whole days ... a daube of succulent and well-basted meats, is surely the greatest of all treasures!

HENRI BOSCO
Barboche

O, scent of the daubes of my childhood!

PIERRE HUGUENIN
Les Meilleures recettes de ma pauvre mère, 1936

An exquisite scent of olives and oil and juice rose from the great brown dish....

VIRGINIA WOOLF
To the Lighthouse

I want to take you to *Chez Clémence*, a small bistro in the rue Vavin, where only one dish is made, but a prodigious one. It is well known that in order to develop its full flavour cassoulet must simmer only on low heat. Mère Clémence's cassoulet has been cooking for twenty years. She adds to the pot, from time to time, some goose, pork fat, perhaps a piece of saucisson or a few beans. But it is always the same cassoulet: the base remains the same – this ancient and precious base which gives the dish the amber toned quality so reminiscent of the old Venetian masters.

    ANATOLE FRANCE
    Histoire comique

Ah, sausage! how fine a thing it is …

    VOLTAIRE
    in a letter to the Marquis d'Albergati

I always think sausages ain't sausages if they ain't stuffed. Aunt Anne won't have the plague of it; but I say, if a thing's worth doing at all, it's worth doing the best way; and there's no comparison in my mind.

    SUSAN WARNER
    Nobody, 1832

Cornwall squab-pie, and Devon white-pot brings;
And Leicester beans and bacon, food of kings.

    WILLIAM KING
    The Art of Cookery, 1708

'It's a stew of tripe,' said the landlord smacking his lips, 'and cow-heel,' smacking them again, 'and bacon,' smacking them once more, 'and steak,' smacking them for the fourth time, 'and peas, cauliflowers, new potatoes, and sparrow-grass [asparagus], all working up together in one delicious gravy.' Having come to the climax, he smacked his lips a great many times, and taking a long hearty sniff of the fragrance that was hovering about, put on the cover again with the air of one whose toils on earth were over.

CHARLES DICKENS
The Old Curiosity Shop

Gently stir and blow the fire,
Lay the mutton down to roast,
Dress it quickly, I desire,
In the dripping put a toast,
That I hunger may remove –
Mutton is the meat I love.

JONATHAN SWIFT

The leg of mutton of Wales beats the leg of mutton of any other country.... Certainly I shall never forget the first Welsh leg of mutton which I tasted, rich but delicate, replete with juices deprived from the aromatic herbs of the noble Berwyn, cooked to a turn and weighing just four pounds.

GEORGE BORROW
Wild Wales

You had all some of the crackling and brown sauce – did you remember to rub it with butter and gently dredge it a little just before the crisis? ... Was the crackling the colour of the ripe pomegranate? ... To confess an honest truth, a pig is one of those things I could never think of sending away.

CHARLES LAMB
Letters

He has lived only to eat, he eats only to die.... His ignoble greed is expiated in a terrible way.... The pig is simply a vast dish walking around until it is time to be served up at table. His pink skin, spotted with black, brings to mind a truffled galantine; his firm and well-padded rump is already the shape of a ham.

XAVIER AUBRYET
La Cuisinière poétique, 1877

Wild boar is sometimes found in the mountains: it has a delicious taste, not unlike that of the wild hog in Jamaica.

TOBIAS SMOLLETT
Travels Through France and Italy, 1766

Here, then, we ate wild boar, shot in the precincts of the mine that very morning, and baked in a ground oven by a Sarde cook. With lettuces, bread, cheese, olives, oranges, wine of Tortoli, and the mountain air, it was a feast for an alderman.

CHARLES EDWARDS
Sardinia and the Sardes, 1889

The capon is above all other foules praised, for as much as it is easily digested.

> SIR THOMAS ELYOT
> *The Castel of Helth*, 1539

He escorted her to the enormous open fire of wood in front of which a row of once-feathered vertebrates were slowly revolving on a horizontal rod.

'We return always to the old methods, mademoiselle,' said he. 'Here in this kitchen we cook by electricity, by gas, by everything you wish, but for the *volaille* we return always to the old methods. Wood fire.'

The intense heat halted Gracie. The master, however, august showman, walked right into it, seized an iron spoon fit for supping with the devil, and having scooped up an immense spoonful of the fat which had dripped drop by drop from the roasting birds, poured it tenderly over them, and so again and again.

> ARNOLD BENNETT
> *Imperial Palace*

A magnificent turkey had just been taken off the spit; a fine specimen, done to a turn and golden brown, its aroma would have tempted a saint.

> BRILLAT-SAVARIN
> *La Physiologie du goût*

'We have just eaten a superb turkey. It was excellent, crammed with truffles up to its beak, tender as a fat pullet, plump as an ortolan, fragrant as a thrush …'

> ALEXANDRE DUMAS
> *La Grand Dictionnaire de cuisine*, 1873

A Michaelmas goose is as famous in the mouths of the million as the minced-pie at Christmas; yet for those who eat with delicacy, it is, at that time, too full-grown. The true period when the goose is in the highest perfection is when it has just acquired its full growth, and not begun to harden; if the March goose is insipid, the Michaelmas goose is rank. The fine time is between both; from the second week in June to the first in September.

> DR WILLIAM KITCHINER
> *The Cook's Oracle*, 1820

When the goose was on the table, huge and golden and running with juices, it was not started on all at once. Everyone was speechless with awe and wonderment. There were winks and nods as they pointed it out to each other. What a devil of a fine fat bird it was – what legs! what a breast!

> EMILE ZOLA
> *L'Assommoir*

All game birds should be roasted on a spit; cooked in the oven they do not have the same succulence. To pretend the contrary is heresy condemned by synods of the fathers of the table.

> LUCIEN TENDRET
> *La Table au pays de Brillat-Savarin*, 1892

Fesaunt exceedeth all foules in sweetnesse and wholesomenesse, and is equal to a capon in nourishment.... It is meate for Princes and great estates, and for poor Schollers when they can get it.

> SIR THOMAS ELYOT
> *The Castel of Helth*, 1539

If there is a pure and elevated pleasure in this world, it is that of roast pheasant and bread sauce; – barn-door fowls for dissenters, but for the real churchmen, the thirty-nine times articled clerk – the pheasant, the pheasant!

REVD SYDNEY SMITH

A pheasant cooked in this way [stuffed with minced woodcock, bacon and good truffles, placed on a slice of bread spread with the woodcocks' livers and pounded truffles, and served surrounded with bitter oranges] would be worthy to set before angels, if they still walked the earth as in the days of Lot.

BRILLAT-SAVARIN
La Physiologie du goût

Serve a duck whole, but eat only the breast and neck; the rest send back to the cook.

MARTIAL
Epigrams

We all know that in spring a young man's fancy lightly turns to thoughts of love, but it is not such common knowledge that in the early summer the thoughts of a man of mature age turn with equal agility to duckling and green peas.

NATHANIEL NEWNHAM-DAVIES
The Gourmet's Guide to London, 1914

Some Epicures like the bird very much underdone, and direct that a Woodcock should just be introduced to the Cook, for her to shew it to the fire, and then send it up to Table.

THOMAS LOVE PEACOCK

Whether woodcock or partridge, what does it signify, if the taste is the same? But the partridge is dearer, and therefore thought preferable.

MARTIAL
Epigrams

If the partridge had the woodcock's thigh
It would be the best bird that ever did fly.

JOHN RAY
English Proverbs

A vine-leaf wrapped round a partridge brings out its quality, just as the barrel of Diogenes brought forth the qualities of the great thinker.

DES ESSARTS
18th-century actor and gastronome

To follow, we were served with a leg of lamb, tender and pink, accompanied by a purée of chestnuts. Then, a surprise ... a huge, sealed terrine was placed in the middle of the table and, when it was uncovered, gave out a marvellous aroma of truffles, partridges and herbs.

This terrine contained eight young partridges, generously truffled and cased in fat bacon, a little bouquet of mountain herbs and several glasses of *fine-champagne* cognac.

AUGUSTE ESCOFFIER
Le Carnet d'Epicure, 1912

All paradise opens! Let me die eating ortolans to the sound of soft music.

BENJAMIN DISRAELI
The Young Duke

As long as I have fat turtle-doves, a fig for your lettuce, my friend … I have no wish to waste my appetite.

    MARTIAL
    Epigrams

Here's a pigeon so finely roasted, it cries, Come, eat me!

    JONATHAN SWIFT
    Polite Conversation

Have I mentioned the quails with rice that one eats in Milan? This dish is what I found most remarkable about the city, and it made the journey worthwhile.

    PROSPER MÉRIMÉE
    Lettre à une inconnue, 1858

28 January 1780 We had for dinner a Calf's Head, boiled Fowl and Tongue, a Saddle of Mutton rosted on the Side Table, and a fine Swan rosted with Currant Jelly Sauce for the first Course. The Second Course a couple of Wild Fowl called Dun Fowls, Larks, Blamange, Tarts etc etc and a good Desert of Fruit after amongst which was a Damson Cheese. I never eat a bit of a Swan before, and I think it good eating with sweet sauce. The Swan was killed 3 weeks before it was eat and yet not the lest bad taste in it.

    JAMES WOODFORDE
    The Diary of a Country Parson

If my opinion is of any worth, the fieldfare is the greatest delicacy among birds, the hare among quadrupeds.

    MARTIAL
    Epigrams

Many are the ways, and many the recipes
For dressing a hare, but this is best of all:
To place before a set of hungry guests
A slice of roasted meat fresh from the spit,
Hot, seasoned only with plain simple salt,
Not too much done. And do you not be vexed,
At seeing blood fresh trickling from the meat,
But eat it eagerly. All other ways
Are quite superfluous, such as when cooks pour
A lot of sticky clammy sauce upon it.
    ARCHESTRATUS

One cut from ven'son to the heart can speak
Stronger than ten quotations from the Greek.
    JOHN WOLCOT
    Bozzy and Piozzi, 1786

For finer or fatter
Never ranged in a forest, or smoked in a platter;
The haunch was a picture for painters to study;
The fat was so white, and the lean was so ruddy.
    OLIVER GOLDSMITH
    'The Haunch of Venison'

A gourmand who had just been appointed tax collector for the Périgueux district was being congratulated by his friends who enthused on the delights of living in that paradise of good food – the country of truffles, partridges and truffled turkey. 'Alas,' said the melancholy gastronome, 'is it possible for a man to live at all in a land where the tide never comes in?'
    BRILLAT-SAVARIN
    La Physiologie du goût

Fish is held out to be one of the greatest luxuries of the table and not only necessary, but even indispensable at all dinners where there is any pretence to excellence or fashion.

ISABELLA BEETON
The Book of Household Management, 1861

Fysshe, the which is in ryvers and brokes, be more holsome than they be in ponds and mootes, or other standing water, for they doeth labour and doth skower themselves. Fysshe that do feede in the fen or morysshe ground doth saver of the moude.

ANDREW BOORDE
A Dyetary of Helth, 1542

What should I speake of the fat and sweet salmon dailie taken in this streame, and that there is such plentie as no river in Europa is able to exceed it. What store also of barbels, trouts ... roches, daces, gudgings, flounders, shrimps....

HOLINSHED
writing of the Thames in *Chronicles*, 1577

Of all the fish in the sea herring is king.

JAMES HOWELL
Proverbs, 17th century

With the exception of *truite au bleu*, nobody knows how to cook a trout. It is the most unfortunate fish on earth.

JEAN GIONO
in *La France à table*

They were such trout as, when once tasted, remain for ever in the recollection of a commonly grateful mind – rich, flaky, creamy, full of flavour. A Parisian *gourmand* would have paid ten francs for the smallest *cooleen* among them; and, when transported to his capital, how different in flavouring they would have been! – how inferior to what they were as we devoured them, fresh from the water to the gridiron!

> W.M. THACKERAY
> *The Irish Sketch Book*

Fish should swim thrice: first it should swim in the sea ... then it should swim in butter, and at last, sirrah, it should swim in good claret.

> JONATHAN SWIFT
> *Polite Conversation*

George knows everything about every fish that comes in here – where they came from, what they were doing before they were caught, who their mothers and fathers were.

> STANLEY KRAMER
> chef of the Grand Central Oyster Bar, New York, about the seafood buyer at the restaurant
> *Manhattan Inc.*, 1984

Fish should smell like the tide. Once they smell like fish, it's too late.

> OSCAR GIZELT
> of Delmonico's restaurant, New York
> *Vogue*, 1964

The Rev. Dr. Folliott: Here is a very fine salmon before me: and May is the very *point nommé* to have salmon in perfection. There is a fine turbot close by, and there is much to be said in his behalf; but salmon in May is the king of fish.

Mr. Crotchet: That salmon before you, doctor, was caught in the Thames this morning.

THOMAS LOVE PEACOCK
Crotchet Castle

… l'Hostellerie du Château at Chaumont-sur-Loire, where the salmon leaps straight out of the water, through the window and into the pan …

BERNARD LEVIN
Enthusiasms

Salmon is a most agreeable fish, most natural boiled, and yet again it is good anyway you like to cook it…. For whole fish, you need big dishes like my master has, because all fish are much better cooked whole rather than in pieces.

MAESTRO MARTINE
De Honesta Voluptate et Valetudine
15th century

However great the dish that holds the turbot, the turbot is still greater than the dish.

MARTIAL
Epigrams

16 May 1781 ... We had the best day of Fishing we ever had. We caught at one draught only ten full Pails of Fish, Pike, Trout and flat fish. The largest Fish we caught was a Pike, which was a Yard long and weighed upwards of thirteen pound after he was brought home ...

17 May 1781 ... I gave my Company for dinner my great Pike which was rosted and a Pudding in his Belly, some boiled Trout, Perch, and Tench, Eel and Gudgeon fryed, a Neck of Mutton boiled and a plain Pudding for Mrs Howes. All my Company were quite astonished at the sight of the great Pike on the table. Was obliged to lay him on two of the largest dishes, and was laid on part of the Kitchen Window shutters, covered with a cloth. I never saw a nobler Fish at any table, it was very well cooked, and tho' so large was declared by all the Company to be prodigious fine eating, being so moist.

> JAMES WOODFORDE
> *The Diary of a Country Parson*

Then a lamprey was brought in, lying on a great platter with shrimp sauce. Our host informed us that it had been caught before spawning, as its meat is less succulent if caught after spawning, and he gave us the recipe for the sauce: 'You need virgin oil from Venafrum; roe and juices from the Spanish mackerel; a domestic wine, five years old, added while the sauce is simmering – Chian is the best wine to use after the sauce is cooked – white pepper, and vinegar produced from fermenting Lesbian wine....'

> HORACE
> *Satires*

He can't get over it. He praises it to the skies. He fills a glass with brandy and drinks a toast to the fish.

SHOLOM ALEICHEM
Tit for Tat

What an idiot is man to believe that abstaining from flesh, and eating fish, which is so much more delicate and delicious, constitutes fasting.

NAPOLEON I

The meal was both frugal and refined. A tureen of crayfish soup had just been removed, and on the table were a salmon-trout, an omelette and a salad.

'My dinner will make it plain,' said the curé with a smile, 'that today – though you may be unaware of the fact – is a day of abstinence according to the rules of the Church.'

BRILLAT-SAVARIN
La Physiologie du goût

Do you really suppose the Almighty takes pleasure in seeing you eat salmon trout rather than boiled beef on a Friday?

FRANÇOIS MAURIAC
Le Nœud de vipères

For the Friday fast the abbess of a Marseilles convent once created the dish of bouillabaisse.

MÉRY
La Cuisinière poétique, 1877

This Bouillabaisse a noble dish is –
A sort of soup, or broth, or brew,
Or hotchpotch of all sorts of fishes,
That Greenwich never could outdo;
Green herbs, red peppers, mussels, saffron,
Soles, onions, garlic, roach, and dace;
All these to eat at Terré's tavern
In that one dish of Bouillabaisse.
W.M. THACKERAY
'Ballad of Bouillabaisse'

You know all sea-birds are allowed by the church of Rome to be eaten on meagre days, as a kind of fish; and the monks especially do not fail to make use of this permission. Sea turtle, or tortoises, are often found at sea by the mariners, in these latitudes: but they are not the green sort, so much in request among the aldermen of London.
TOBIAS SMOLLETT
Travels Through France and Italy, 1766

Of all the things I ever swallow,
Good well-dress'd turtle beats them hollow …
THOMAS HOOD
'The Turtles'

Porpoises are indeed to this day considered fine eating. The meat is made into balls about the size of billiard balls, and being well seasoned and spiced might be taken for turtle-balls or veal balls. The old monks of Dumferline were very fond of them. They had a great porpoise grant from the crown.
HERMAN MELVILLE
Moby Dick

Once taste porpoise and all other food will seem insipid.
CHINESE PROVERB

I am ready to defend the right of the tasty crab, the luscious oyster, the noble rockfish and the incomparable terrapin to continue their part in the penitential practice of Friday.
CARDINAL SHEHAN, Archbishop of Baltimore
New York Times, January 1966

A crabbe, breke hym a-sonder in a dysshe, make ye shelle cleane and put him in the stuffe againe; tempre it with vynegre and pouder, then cover it with brede, and send it to the kytchyn to hete; then set it to your soverayne, and breke the grete clawes, and laye them in a disshe.
WYNKYN DE WORDE
Boke of Kervynge

What good are vitamins? Eat four lobsters, eat a pound of caviar – live!
ARTHUR RUBINSTEIN

I've never heard of anyone being tired of eating lobster.
JANE GRIGSON
Good Things

All the ingenious men and all the scientific men, and all the imaginative men in the world could never invent, if all their wits were boiled into one, anything so curious and so ridiculous as a lobster.
CHARLES KINGSLEY
The Water Babies

An oyster, that marvel of delicacy, that concentration of sapid excellence, that mouthful before all other mouthfuls, who first had faith to believe it, and courage to execute? The exterior is not persuasive.

> HENRY WARD BEECHER
> *Eyes and Ears*

Oysters are the usual opening to a winter breakfast ... indeed they are almost indispensable.

> GRIMOD DE LA REYNIÈRE
> *Almanach des Gourmands*

Oysters are amatory food.

> BYRON
> *Don Juan*

It is proven by experience that, above five or six dozen, oysters cease to be a pleasure.

> GRIMOD DE LA REYNIÈRE
> *Almanach des Gourmands*

I ate the oysters with their strong taste of the sea and their faint metallic taste that the cold white wine washed away, leaving only the sea taste and the succulent texture....

> ERNEST HEMINGWAY
> *A Moveable Feast*

Practically all the littleneck and cherrystone clams served on the half shell in New York restaurants come out of the black mud of Long Island bays. They are the saltiest, cleanest, and biggest-bellied clams in the world.

> JOSEPH MITCHELL
> *McSorley's Wonderful Saloon*

There is an Italian sauce called *caviaro*, which begins to be in use with us, such vain affectors are we of novelties. It is prepared of the spawn of the sturgeon: the very name doth well express its nature, that it is good to beware of it.

> DR TOBIAS VENNER
> *Via recta ad vitam longam*, 1620

… an ounce of caviare rolled in smoked salmon will produce mumbles of ecstasy.

> ANDRÉ LAUNAY
> *Caviare and After*

Our people esteem the goose chiefly on account of the excellence of the liver, which attains a very large size when the bird is crammed. When the liver is thoroughly soaked in honey and milk, it becomes specially large.

> PLINY THE ELDER

Thou most beautiful of all, thou evening star of entremets – thou that delightest in truffles, and gloriest in a dark cloud of sauces – exquisite foie gras! – Have I forgotten thee? Do I not, on the contrary, see thee, smell thee, taste thee, and almost die with rapture of thy possession?

> EDWARD BULWER-LYTTON
> *Pelham*

There is nothing much better in the Western world than a fine, unctuous, truffled pâté.

> M.F.K. FISHER
> *An Alphabet for Gourmets*

Thy truffles, Perigord! thy hams, Bayonne!
>   ALEXANDER POPE
>   *The Dunciad*

Presently we were aware of an odour gradually coming towards us, something musky, fiery, savoury, mysterious – a hot, drowsy smell, that lulls the senses and yet enflames them – the truffles were coming.
>   W.M. THACKERAY
>   *Memorials of Gourmandising*

The truffle is the diamond of cookery.
>   BRILLAT-SAVARIN
>   *La Physiologie du goût*

... the ambrosia of the gods, the *sacrum sacrorum* of gastronomes.
>   ALEXANDRE DUMAS
>   *Le Grand Dictionnaire de cuisine*

We have potatoes from the mountains, mushrooms, champignons, and truffles. Piedmont affords *white truffles*, counted the most delicious in the world; they sell for about three livres the pound.
>   TOBIAS SMOLLETT
>   *Travels Through France and Italy*, 1766

Away with all this slicing, this dicing, this grating, this peeling of truffles! ... Eat it like the vegetable it is, hot and served in munificent quantities.
>   COLETTE
>   *Prisons et paradis*

Those who wish to lead virtuous lives should abstain from truffles.

OLD FRENCH PROVERB

Asparagus ... being taken fasting several mornings together, stirreth up bodily lust in man or woman, whatever some have written to the contrary.

NICHOLAS CULPEPER
Complete Herbal

At the end of this month [April] one sees the points of asparagus emerge, something which brings a great consolation to those who, tired of potatoes and dried cereals, long for something green.

GRIMOD DE LA REYNIÈRE
Almanach des gourmands

Great care must be taken to watch the exact time of their [asparagus] becoming tender; take them just at that instant, and they will have their true flavour and colour; a minute or two more boiling destroys both.

MARY RANDOLPH
The Virginia House-wife, 1824

Most people spoil garden things by over boiling them. All things that are green should have a little crispness, for if they are overboil'd they neither have any sweetness or beauty.

HANNAH GLASSE
The Art of Cookery, 1747

The artichoke is, after all, an extremely civilized thistle with a very gastronomic beginning.
ANDRÉ LAUNAY
Caviare and After

A cook capable of preparing a plate of chard to perfection has the right to call himself the finest artist in Europe.
GRIMOD DE LA REYNIÈRE
Almanach des gourmands

Gave up spinach for Lent.
F. SCOTT FITZGERALD

You need to have the soul of a rabbit to eat lettuce as it is usually served.... A salad is only a background; it needs embroidering.
PAUL REBOUX

Lettuce, like conversation, requires a good deal of oil, to avoid friction, and keep the company smooth.
CHARLES DUDLEY WARNER
My Summer in a Garden, 1871

According to the Spanish proverb, four persons are wanted to make a good salad: a spendthrift for oil, a miser for vinegar, a counsellor for salt, and a madman to stir all up.
ABRAHAM HAYWARD
The Art of Dining

What is more refreshing than salads when your appetite seems to have deserted you, or even after a capacious dinner – the nice, fresh, green, and crisp salad, full of life and health, which seems to invigorate the palate.

ALEXIS SOYER
A Shilling Cookery for the People

Two large potatoes, passed through kitchen sieve,
Unwonted softness to the salad give;
Of mordent mustard, add a single spoon,
Distrust the condiment which bites too soon;
But deem it not, thou man of herbs, a fault,
To add a double quantity of salt;
Three times the spoon with oil of Lucca crown,
And once with vinegar, procured from town;
True flavour needs it, and your poet begs
The pounded yellow of two well-boiled eggs;
Let onion atoms lurk within the bowl,
And scarce suspected, animate the whole
And lastly, in the flavoured compound toss
A magic teaspoon of anchovy sauce:
Then, though green turtle fail, though venison's tough,
And ham and turkey are not boiled enough,
Serenely full, the epicure may say –
Fate cannot harm me – I have dined today.

REVD SYDNEY SMITH
'Receipt for Salad'

The apple was the first fruit of the world, according to Genesis, but it was no Cox's orange pippin. God gave the crab apple and left the rest to man.
JANE GRIGSON
Jane Grigson's Fruit Book

An apple is an excellent thing – till you have tried a peach.
GEORGE DU MAURIER
Trilby

Raw crayme undecocted, eaten with strawberys or hurtes [whortleberries] is a rurall mannes banket. I have knowne such bankettes hath put men in jeopardy of they lyves.
ANDREW BOORDE
A Dyetary of Helth, 1542

... the triple alliance of strawberries, champagne, and whipped cream.
MAURICE GERMA
La Cuisinière poétique, 1877

Strawberries, and only strawberries, could now be thought or spoken of. 'The best fruit in England – everybody's favourite – always wholesome. These the finest beds and finest sorts. Delightful to gather for oneself – the only way of really enjoying them. Morning decidedly the best time – never tired – every sort good – hautboy infinitely superior – no comparison.'
JANE AUSTEN
Emma

Talking of Pleasure, this moment I was writing with one hand, and with the other holding to my Mouth a Nectarine – good god, how fine. It went down soft, pulpy, slushy, oozy – all its delicious *embonpoint* melted down my throat like a large beatified Strawberry. I shall certainly breed.

> JOHN KEATS
> in a letter to Charles Dilke

Ripe Apples drop about my head,
The Luscious Clusters of the Vine
Upon my mouth do crush their Wine;
The Nectaren, and curious Peach,
Into my hands themselves do reach;
Stumbling on Melons, as I pass....

> ANDREW MARVELL
> 'The Garden'

From this immense sea of green leaves rose a number of plum, pear, orange, and apricot trees; the latter procured by the monks directly from Damascus, and bearing that most delicious fruit of its kind called 'eggs of the sun' by the Persians; – even insects and worms seem to respect it, for no trace could I discover of their having preyed on its smooth glowing rind and surrounding foliage.

> WILLIAM BECKFORD
> *Travel Diaries*

The flesh of the pineapple melts into water and it is so flavourful that one finds in it the aroma of the peach, the apple, the quince and the muscat grape. I can call it with justice the king of fruits because it is the most beautiful and best of all those of the earth.

> PÈRE DU TERTRE
> 16th century

The brave fellow had bought several dozen of those mangosteens, crimson red inside, whose white flesh melts in the mouth and gives true gourmets incomparable pleasure.

> JULES VERNE
> *Le Tour du monde en 80 jours*

Blueberries as big as the end of your thumb,
Real sky-blue, and heavy, and ready to drum
In the cavernous pail of the first one to come!

> ROBERT FROST

The greatest fault I find with most fruits in this climate is that they are too sweet and luscious and want that agreeable acid which is so cooling and so grateful in a hot country. This, too, is the case with our grapes, of which there is great plenty and variety, plump and juicy, and large as plumbs. Nature, however, has not neglected to provide other agreeable vegetable juices to cool the human body. During the whole summer, we have plenty of musk melons. I can buy one as large as my head for the value of an English penny.

> TOBIAS SMOLLETT
> *Travels Through France and Italy*, 1766

Women, melons and cheese should be chosen by weight.

> SPANISH PROVERB

Gooseberry pie is best;
Full of the theme, O Muse, begin the song! ...
The flour, the sugar, and the fruit,
Commingled well, how well they suit!
And they were well bestow'd.
O Jane, with truth I praise your pie,
And will you not, in just reply,
Praise my Pindaric ode?
    ROBERT SOUTHEY
    'An Ode to Gooseberry Pie'

Of all the delicates which Britons try
To please the palate or delight the eye,
Of all the sev'ral kinds of sumptuous fare,
There is none that can with applepie compare.
Ranged in thick order let your Quinces be,
They give a charming relish to the Pie.
If you are wise you'll not brown sugar slight,
The browner (if I form my judgment right)
A deep vermilion tincture will dispense,
And make your Pippin redder than the Quince ...
O be not, be not tempted, lovely Nell!
While the hot-piping odours strongly smell,
While the delicious fume creates a gust,
To lick the o'erflowing juice or bite the crust.
    WILLIAM KING
    The Art of Cookery, 1708

An apple-pie without some cheese
Is like a kiss without a squeeze.
    OLD ENGLISH RHYME

Your cheese is the best I ever tasted. Mary ... has sense
enough to value your present; for she is very fond of Stilton.
Yours is the delicatest, rainbow-hued, melting piece I ever
flavoured.
> CHARLES LAMB
> in a letter to Thomas Allsop, 1823

Brie alone deserves to have her praises recorded in letters of
gold.
> SAINT-AMANT
> 17th-century French poet

The blood-red fruitage of a summer's day,
The Autumn orchard's gold and purple spoil,
Gleam here, encrystalled by the tropic cane.
> EPICURUS

And still she slept, an azure-lidded sleep,
In blanched linen, smooth and lavender'd,
While he from forth the closet brought a heap
Of candied apple, quince, and plum, and gourd:
With jellies soother than the creamy curd,
And lucent syrops, tinct with cinnamon;
Manna and dates, in argosy transferr'd
From Fez; and spiced dainties, every one,
From silken Samarkand to cedared Lebanon.
> JOHN KEATS
> 'The Eve of St Agnes'

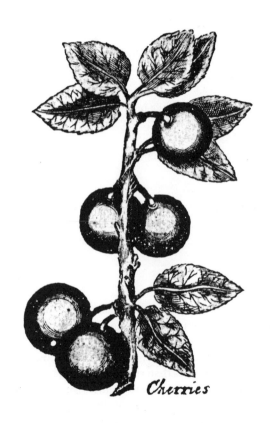

Cherries

Attic honey thickens the nectar-like Falernian.
Such drink deserves to be mixed by Ganymede.
> MARTIAL
> *Epigrams*

Honey is too good for a bear.
> THOMAS FULLER
> *Gnomologia*

My son, eat thou honey, because it is good.
> PROVERBS, 24:13

And is there honey still for tea?
> RUPERT BROOKE
> 'The Old Vicarage, Grantchester'

… the ample charms of a genuine Dutch country tea table, in the sumptuous time of autumn. Such heaped-up platters of cakes of various and almost indescribable kinds.… There was the doughty doughnut, the tenderer oly koek, and the crisp and crumbling cruller; sweet cakes and shortcakes, ginger cakes and honey cakes.… And then there were apple pies and peach pies and pumpkin pies; beside slices of ham and smoked beef; and moreover delectable dishes of preserved plums, and peaches, and pears, and quinces … together with bowls of milk and cream, all mingled higgledy-piggledy … with the motherly teapot sending up its clouds of vapor from the midst.
> WASHINGTON IRVING
> *The Legend of Sleepy Hollow*

Though we eat little flesh and drink no wine,
Yet let's be merry: we'll have tea and toast;
Custards for supper, and an endless host
Of syllabubs and jellies and mince-pies,
And other such lady-like luxuries.
> P.B. SHELLEY
> 'Letter to Maria Gisborne'

'Well, Sire, with regard to sweet dishes, I recognize only pastry, and even that should be rather solid; all these frothy substances swell my stomach, and occupy a space which seems to me to be too precious to be so badly tenanted.'
> ALEXANDRE DUMAS
> *Le Vicomte de Bragelonne*
> Porthos to Louis XIV

They eat and drank deeply of the charming viands ending up with merangs and chocolates.
> DAISY ASHFORD
> *The Young Visiters*

My tongue is smiling.
> ABIGAIL TRILLIN
> aged four, after eating chocolate ice-cream, quoted by her father, Calvin Trillin, in *Alice, Let's Eat*

Huge blond *babas, Mont Blancs* snowy with whipped cream, cakes speckled with white almonds and green pistachio nuts, hillocks of chocolate-covered pastry....
> GIUSEPPE DI LAMPEDUSA
> *The Leopard*

... an astounding dessert that consisted of no more than unfermented goat's cheese from the farm next door with white *armagnac* beaten into it....
>BERNARD LEVIN
>*Enthusiasms*

The ultimate cheesecake? Rich, delicate, subtly flavored ... a litany of all the pleasures of which cream is capable.
>JOHN THORNE
>*Simple Cooking*

The Poor Author's Pudding
New milk, 1 quart; cinnamon, or lemon-rind; sugar, 3 oz; little salt; eggs, 3; buttered bread: baked ½ hour ...

The Publisher's Pudding
This pudding can scarcely be made *too* rich ...
Jordan almonds, 6oz; bitter almonds, 12; cream, ¾ pint; bread-crumbs, 4oz; cream wrung from almonds, ½ pint; crushed maccaroons, 4oz; flour, 2oz; beef-suet, 5oz; marrow, 5oz; dried cherries, 4oz; stoned muscatel raisins, 4oz; pounded sugar, 6oz; candied citron (or citron and orange-rind mixed), ½lb; pinch of salt; ½ nutmeg; grated rind, 1 lemon; yolks of eggs, 7; best cognac, 1 wineglassful: boiled in mould or basin, 4 ¼ hours.
>ELIZA ACTON
>*Modern Cookery for Private Families*, 1845

To eat well in England you should have breakfast three times a day.
>attributed to SOMERSET MAUGHAM

The tea consumed was the very best, the coffee the very blackest, the cream the very thickest; there was dry toast and buttered toast, muffins and crumpets; hot bread and cold bread, white bread and brown bread, home-made bread and bakers' bread, wheaten bread and oaten bread.... There were eggs in napkins, and crispy bits of bacon under silver covers; and there were little fishes in a little box, and devilled kidneys frizzling on a hot-water dish.... Such was the ordinary fare at Plumstead Episcopi.

> ANTHONY TROLLOPE
> *The Warden*

Waverley found Miss Bradwardine presiding over the tea and coffee, the table loaded with warm bread, both of flour, oatmeal and barley meal, in the shape of loaves, cakes, biscuits and other varieties, together with eggs, reindeer ham ... smoked salmon, marmalade and all the other delicacies which induced even Johnson himself to extol the luxury of a Scottish breakfast above that of all other countries. A mess of oatmeal porridge, flanked by a silver jug, which held an equal mixture of cream and buttermilk, was placed for the Baron's share of this repast.

> SIR WALTER SCOTT
> *Waverley*

Well-made porridge with brown sugar and cream is a dish fit for a king.

> IRIS MURDOCH
> *The Sea, The Sea*

Bring porridge, bring sausage, bring fish for a start,
Bring kidneys and mushrooms and partridge's legs.
But let the foundation be bacon and eggs.

>A.P. HERBERT
>'Breakfast'

What a breakfast! Pot of hare; ditto of trout; pot of prepared
shrimps; tin of sardines; beautiful beefsteak; eggs, mutton,
large loaf and butter, not forgetting capital tea.

>GEORGE BORROW
>*Wild Wales*

Life, within doors, has few pleasanter prospects than a
neatly arranged and well provisioned breakfast-table.

>NATHANIEL HAWTHORNE
>*The House of the Seven Gables*

Everything tastes better outdoors.

>CLAUDIA RODEN
>*Picnic*

In ample space under the broadest shade,
A table richly spread in regal mode,
With dishes piled and meats of noblest sort
And savour – beasts of chase, or fowl of game,
In pastry built, or from the spit, or boiled,
Gris-amber-steamed; all fish, from sea or shore,
Freshet or purling brook, of shell or fin
And exquisitest name....

>JOHN MILTON
>*Paradise Lost*

There was a *pâté de Périgord*, over which a gastronome would have wished to live and die, like Homer's lotus-eaters, forgetful of kin, native country, and all social obligations whatever. Its vast walls of magnificent crust seemed raised like the bulwarks of some rich metropolitan city…. There was a delicate ragout, with just that *petit point de l'ail* which Gascons love, and Scottishmen do not hate. There was, besides, a delicate ham, which had once supported a noble wild boar in the neighbouring wood of Mountrichart. There was the most exquisite white bread, made into little round loaves called *boules* (whence the bakers took their French name of *boulangers*), of which the crust was so inviting, that, even with water alone, it would have been a delicacy. But the water was not alone, for there was a flask of leather called *bottrine*, which contained about a quart of exquisite *Vin de Beaulne*.

SIR WALTER SCOTT
Quentin Durward

A shooting party luncheon: Filets de Soles à la mayonnaise, Mousse de Homard frappé, Bœuf braisé à la gelée, Langue à l'écarlate, Filets de Caneton à la Lorraine, Cailles poéllées à la Parisienne, Faisan en Robe de Chambre, Salade à la Japonaise, Bordure de Riz aux Prunes, Gâteaux à l'Africaine, Bâtons Gruyère, Fromage, Dessert.

ISABELLA BEETON
The Book of Household Management, 1861

A picnic at Snodhill
21 June 1870 There was plenty of meat and drink, the usual
things, cold chicken, ham and tongue, pies of different
sorts, salads, jam and gooseberry tarts, bread and cheese.
Splendid strawberries from Clifford Priory brought by the
Haigh Allens. Cup of various kinds went round, claret and
hock, champagne, cider and sherry, and people sprawled
about in all attitudes and made a great noise.

> REVD FRANCIS KILVERT
> *Diary*

Boule de Suif ... pulled out from under the seat a large
basket covered with a white napkin.

She took out first a small plate and a silver goblet, then a
huge terrine in which two whole chickens, cut up into
pieces, were nestling in jelly; and one could see other good
things wrapped up in the basket, pâtés, fruit and other
delicacies, everything needed for a three-day journey so as
not to have to eat at the inns on the way.... She picked up
a chicken wing, and delicately began to eat it.

All eyes were turned towards her. The aroma filled the
coach, making nostrils flare and mouths water.

> GUY DE MAUPASSANT
> *Boule de Suif*

Lunch was just ending. The landlord ... said that we were
unfortunately too late for a proper lunch, but they would
see what they could do for us. Here is what they did for us:
Soupe, Jambon du pays, Confit d'oie, Omelette nature,
Civet de lièvre, Riz de veau blanquette, Perdreau rôti,
Fromage Roquefort, Fromage Cantal, Confiture de cerise,
Poires, Figues. We ate everything; every dish was really

distinguished.... In addition there were three wines.... The total bill, for two persons, was seven francs.

> ARNOLD BENNETT
> *Things that Have Interested Me*

... gourmets, eternally engaged in a never-ending search for that imaginary, perfect, unknown little back-street bistro....

> ROY ANDRIES DE GROOT
> *Esquire*, May 1970

At a restaurant entitled the Chapon Fin, I had one of the most wondrous meals of my existence as an eater. And not too dear. Poitiers is only a small town, and yet the largeish restaurant was full of lunchers all doing themselves exceedingly well; and few tourists among them. Of the few tourists the most astonishing were two English or Scottish sisters. They ate at length, and never spoke to one another. One had a book and the other a newspaper. They ate truly distinguished food, dish after dish – and they read.

> ARNOLD BENNETT
> *Journals*, July 1929

Midnight Mass
'Two truffled turkeys, Garrigou?' ...

'Yes, reverend father, two magnificent turkeys stuffed with truffles. I know, because I helped to fill them. Fit to burst, they looked ...'

'Jesus! ... Quick, my surplice, Garrigou.... And what else did you see in the kitchen? ...'

'Oh, all sorts of good things.... Since midday we have been busy plucking pheasants, partridges, grouse.... Then some eels and golden carp were brought in from the pool, and trout....'

'How big were the trout, Garrigou?'

'As big as this, reverend father.... Simply enormous!' ...

His mind already troubled by these gastronomic delights, Dom Balaguère repeated to himself as he put his surplice on: 'Roasted turkeys ... golden carp ... simply enormous trout!' ...

So vivid was the vision of these marvels that it seemed as though they were being served up to him on the altar cloth, and two or three times instead of *Dominus vobiscum* he found himself saying the *Benedicite*.

> ALPHONSE DAUDET
> *Les Trois Messes basses*

The table was literally loaded with good cheer, and presented an epitome of country abundance, in this season of overflowing larders. A distinguished post was allotted to 'ancient sirloin', as mine host termed it; being, as he added, 'the standard of old English hospitality, and a joint of goodly presence'.

> WASHINGTON IRVING
> *Old Christmas*

At Ambergate my sister had sent a motorcar for us – so we were at Ripley in time for turkey and Christmas pudding. My God, what masses of food here, turkey, large tongues, long wall of roast loin of pork, pork-pies, sausages, mince-pies, dark cakes covered with almonds, cheese-cakes, lemon-tarts, jellies, endless masses of food, with whisky, gin, port wine, burgundy, muscatel. It seems incredible.

> D.H. LAWRENCE
> in a letter to Katherine Mansfield, 27 December 1918

Heaped up on the floor ... were turkeys, geese, game, poultry, brawn, great joints of meat, sucking-pigs, long wreaths of sausages, mince-pies, plum-puddings, barrels of oysters, red-hot chestnuts, cherry-cheeked apples, juicy oranges, luscious pears, immense twelfth-cakes, and seething bowls of punch that made the chamber dim with their delicious steam.

    CHARLES DICKENS
    A Christmas Carol

4 September 1783 ... There were 20 of us at the Table and a very elegant Dinner the Bishop gave us. We had 2 Courses of 20 Dishes each Course, and a Desert after of 20 Dishes. Madeira, red and white Wines. The first Course amongst many other things were 2 Dishes of prodigious fine stewed Carp and Tench, and a fine Haunch of Venison. Amongst the second Course a fine Turkey Poult, Partridges, Pidgeons and Sweatmeats. Desert – amongst other things, Mulberries, Melon, Currants, Peaches, Nectarines and Grapes.

    JAMES WOODFORDE
    The Diary of a Country Parson

4 April 1663 Very merry before, at, and after dinner, and the more for that my dinner was great and most neatly dressed by our own only mayde. We had a Fricasse of rabbits and chicken – a leg of mutton boiled – three carps in a dish – a great dish of a side of lamb – a dish roasted pigeons – a dish of four lobsters – three tarts – a Lampry pie, a most rare pie – a dish of anchoves – good wine of several sorts; and all things mighty noble and to my great content.

    SAMUEL PEPYS
    Diary

Tio Pepe	Consommé
———	———
Meursault, 1870	Grilse
———	———
Champagne Pommery Extra Sec, 1876	Filets de Soles Ravigotte
	———
	Côtelettes de Mouton Soubise
———	———
Still Red Verzenay, 1868	Chaudfroid de Volaille
	———
	Vol-au-vent Financière
	———
	Virginian Quails
———	———
Gold Dry Sherry	Soufflé glacé au Chocolat
———	———
Ch. Lafite, 1862	Canapés d'Anchois au Fromage

An early (1884), and I think not bad dinner, particularly as regards the wine, though the Claret might have been better. Perhaps the chaudfroid ... and the vol-au-vent come, in both senses, too close together. But I remember how good the still red Verzenay was with the Virginian Quails.

GEORGE SAINTSBURY
Notes on a Cellar-Book

As she entered, Emma was aware of the warm atmosphere in which the scent of flowers, the freshness of fine linen, and the delicious aroma of meats and truffles mingled.
GUSTAVE FLAUBERT
Madame Bovary

Without a liqueur and a coffee the best of meals ends as tamely as a pretty mermaid.
H. WARNER ALLEN
Through the Wine-Glass

Coffee:
Black as the devil,
Hot as hell,
Pure as an angel,
Sweet as love.
TALLEYRAND

Coffee: Inspires wit. Good only if it comes through Le Havre. After a large dinner party it is taken standing up. Take it without sugar – very sophisticated: gives the impression you have lived in the East.
GUSTAVE FLAUBERT
Dictionnaire des idées reçues

The servants carry in large coffee trays decorated with painted flowers, and bearing steaming pewter pots, gleaming, golden Dresden china cups, and tiny jugs of cream. There is no coffee like the Polish coffee.

ADAM MICKIEWICZ
Pan Tadeusz

A cup of coffee – real coffee – home-browned, home-ground, home made, that comes to you dark as a hazel-eye, but changes to a golden bronze as you temper it with cream that never cheated, but was real cream from its birth, thick, tenderly yellow, perfectly sweet ...: such a cup of coffee is a match for twenty blue devils, and will exorcise them all.

HENRY WARD BEECHER
Eyes and Ears

Brandy: The Essence of the Essence of the Grape.

MARTIN ARMSTRONG

Indeed, I think '51 was the finest port, of what may be called the older vintages accessible to my generation, that I ever tasted ... '51 in all its phases, dry, rich and medium, was, I think, such a wine as deserved the famous and pious encomium (slightly altered) that the Almighty might no doubt have caused a better wine to exist, but that he never did.

GEORGE SAINTSBURY
Notes on a Cellar-Book

If I drink water while this doth last,
May I never again drink wine:
For how can a man, in his life of a span,
Do anything better than dine?
We'll dine and drink, and say if we think
That anything better can be;
And when we have dined, wish all mankind
May dine as well as we.
    THOMAS LOVE PEACOCK

If Providence should put a good cigar your way, be thankful
and blow rings of white smoke towards Heaven.
    LUCIEN TENDRET
    La Table au pays de Brillat-Savarin